SUCCESS

Is A

TEAM

EFFORT

SUCCESS
Is A
TEAM
EFFORT

By Charles B. Dygert, Ph.D.

Keene Publishing
Warwick, New York

SUCCESS IS A TEAM EFFORT

QUANTITY PURCHASES
Companies, professional groups, nonprofits, and other organizations may qualify for special discounts when ordering quantities of this title. For information, write Special Sales, Keene Publishing, PO Box 54 Warwick, NY 10990, call 845-987-7750 or email to info@KeeneBooks.com.

Publisher's Cataloging-in-Publication Data
Dygert, Charles B.
 Success is a team effort/ Charles B. Dygert
 — Warwick, N.Y. : Keene Publishing, 2007.
 p. ; cm.
First published: Columbus, OH : Motivational Enterprises, Inc., 1996.
Includes bibliographical references. ISBN: 0-884182-00-3
1. Organizational behavior. 2. Success. 3. Management. 4. Corporate culture.
5. Organizational change. 6. Success in business. I. Dygert, Charles B. II. Title.

HD58.7 .D94   2007   2007111729   658—dc22 0407

Printed in the United States of America.

10 9 8 7 6 5 4 3 2 1

Dedicated to my family
for their patience, love, and support
during the preparation of this book.

—CBD

Contents

Introduction

Recently, after presenting a seminar to a national trade association, I was asked, "Dr. Dygert, what do you consider to be the most important elements of a successful organization?"

I didn't have to think long about the answer. "Teamwork and cooperation," I replied.

In my travels as a consultant and speaker for business, education, and government I have examined the structure of dozens of organizations. I've seen leadership styles that range from being a tyrant to being a teddy-bear—and everything in between.

Transforming the workplace from an autocratic climate to one of harmony and cooperation doesn't happen overnight. It is the result of an intentional effort based on knowledge and a specific plan.

In this book you'll learn the answers to these questions:

- Why do people lose their natural born creativity?
- What is the source of noncooperative thinking?
- How can we build a democratic environment?
- How can the "seven intelligences" be used in building teams?
- What does research tell us about beta endorphins and supportive environments?
- Can stress be a positive influence?
- What can we learn about teamwork from Japan and the former Soviet Union?
- How can we move from conformity to opportunity?
- What are the requirements for building a participative work environment?

As we move further into the 21st century I believe it is possible for mutual respect, common goals, and shared efforts to become the hallmark of society. It is vital for our families, schools, corporations, and government.

Take this opportunity to learn *how* it works, why it works, and what it takes to *make* it work for you and those with whom you associate.

Success is not a game of solitaire, it's a team effort.

1
Democracy at Work

For years I have wrestled with several questions:

- How can we eliminate mistrust among the various layers of an organization?
- Why has the workplace become "mindless drudgery" for millions of formerly creative people?
- What can we do to replace competition with cooperation?
- How can we spend billions of dollars on education and see national test scores sink to record lows?

As an educator, corporate trainer, and public speaker I have seen the problems we face up close. They're not just America's problems in general. They are yours and mine, specifically.

This book has grown out of a belief that it is time for a major revolution in our approach to success. We must say a final farewell to the "me" generation and replace it with "we." My own experience has confirmed that "team building" is more than just an idle phrase. It is a practical, proven strategy that can transform your life—and those around you—into new levels of achievement.

Winners and Losers

We were born in what is called "the world's greatest democracy," but for many that would be hard to believe. The environment of the average organization is anything but democratic. It's more like a dictatorship. Or what we call an autocratic leadership style.

When an urgent situation requires immediate response, autocratic leadership makes sense. Troops fighting a battle, firefighters trying to save lives, police trying to evacuate a flood zone—all are good examples of situations that require an autocratic leadership style.

But in a day-to-day working environment, autocratic management makes very little sense. Autocratic, domineering, controlled atmospheres stifle achievement, destroy self-worth, diminish morale, and impede human progress.

At the heart of an autocratic environment is competition. All our lives we've been conditioned to compete. At home, parents brag about the son or daughter who is "best." Schools pit students against one another in sports and grades. On the job, management creates programs and measurements that create champions and failures. As Daniel Burrus once said,

The focus on competition has always been a formula for mediocrity.

Autocratic leadership stimulates competition and diviseness among those being led. To please a domineering leader, employees will do whatever it takes—including pushing co-workers aside to gain favor with the leader.

Ultimately, individual employees struggling for approval and self-survival are no longer concerned with excellence for the organization. In business, this translates to poor quality of goods and services.

We are born with a healthy quota of natural creativity. How else could we learn a language from scratch, develop our motor skills, and mold our personalities? But why do so many creative fires seem to burn out by the time we're ready to start our careers?

Here's what behavioral research tells us:

*At the age of five we still have
all of our natural creativity,
but by the time we are seven
we have only ten percent of it left.*

What happens during those two crucial years? For one thing, we enter grade school.

If you didn't encounter a domineering, autocratic environment in your home, you probably did when you entered first grade. It was there that you more than likely faced the stark reality of a competitive world. You were thrown into a rivalry with the other pupils, and for many it was where serious problems began.

Contrary to what we would like to believe, the first grade environment was not one of teamwork. You were on your own. If you are a creative person—as most people are—you were in an atmosphere you were not prepared for.

In kindergarten, you learned songs, dances, colors and shapes that helped develop your originality. But in first grade something drastic happened—you entered the world of the "three R's." Your creative intelligence was irrelevant, or at best incidental, to the tasks you were given. You had to make it on your logical skills. And those were the skills you had failed to develop in the home.

If we lose ninety percent of our natural-born creativity by the age of seven, do we get it back? Hardly. By the time we are forty, we're likely to have lost ninety-nine percent of it.

What has happened? Is it because we went to college? Is it because we entered the workplace?

Out of the Frying Pan

The time from graduation to our first job is what someone must have been thinking about when they said, "out of the frying pan and into the fire." That's because the American work place often replicates the autocratic environment already encountered in many homes and in most schools.

Some companies are operated according to the old Prussian military chain of command. Decisions are made at the top, transmitted through the middle, and executed at the bottom.

The "line workers" are like those doomed soldiers in the light brigade, immortalized by Alfred Lord Tennyson:

> *Theirs not to make reply,*
> *Theirs not to reason why,*
> *Theirs but to do and die.*

And where were these brave men headed?

> *Unto the jaws of death,*
> *Into the mouth of hell.*

The men Tennyson was writing about were not born with the willingness to follow orders without question to their deaths. It had to be drummed into them on the drill field. Their native creative intellect had to be suppressed.

When the same thing happens at the factory or in the corporation, we end up with a working population characterized by what has been called "conditioned, noncooperative thinking." It is the lowest of the levels of thinking styles identified in the American workplace and is typically found in domineering environments.

People who reason in this style do so because they have never been given a piece of the decision-making process. Nobody has ever asked them for an opinion. More than one worker has heard a boss say, "It's my way or the highway."

Furthermore, when you're conditioned to think noncooperatively, you eventually reach the point where you really don't *want* a piece of the action. You want somebody to tell you exactly what to do, and then leave you alone.

Noncooperative thinking results from autocratic leadership by people with virtually no management skills.

A manager without previous leadership experience is in a desperate search for role models. Training our managers helps, but more often than not, new managers will fall back on the leadership models they had at home and school.

In the home, parental law is supreme. Therefore, in the workplace, management's law is supreme. That is why so many managers treat their workers like children.

Across our nation we have rule-makers punishing rule-breakers, turning the workforce into thoughtless robots. The employees don't think, or don't want to think, beyond their individual tasks. For them, the company doesn't exist; only the workbench does. As one worker told me, "If I do my job and stay out of trouble, the boss will leave me alone and on payday I'll get my check."

Is it any wonder that our national spirit has been zapped? Should we be surprised that young people are failing to reach our expectations? Are we really shocked that millions have lost their self-esteem and have sought the escape of drugs or alcohol?

The Drive to Succeed

In the home, in education, and on the job, there are usually two options for our environment: *democratic* or *autocratic*. A balance between the two would be welcome, but unfortunately, far too many have opted for the second choice.

It makes little sense that we would choose to create a domineering, controlled atmosphere that inhibits and impedes human progress. Do we really want to destroy self-worth and diminish morale? I don't believe we do. But most people have never acquired the skills necessary to make democracy work on a personal level.

We desire the *results* of a democratic environment but don't seem to know how to achieve it. We would love to replace competition with cooperation, if we just knew how to make it happen.

The high achiever, as we all know, is someone who is motivated. But what is the source of their drive? What makes them pursue a specific goal or object?

Motivation is not a learned skill. It is simply the response to an environment.

The influences and circumstances of your life either "turn you off" or "turn you on." The facts are that people who are motivated are responding to their environments, and people who are *not* motivated are also responding to their environments.

There is a basic reason people attempt to achieve. It serves five specific needs in the human psyche:

- The need for recognition
- The need for economic security

- The need for emotional security
- The need for self-expression
- The need for self-respect

Psychologists Bradford Wilson and George Edington, authors of *First Child, Second Child,* believe people operate according to the natural motivations "to obtain rewards and recognition, to avoid pain and danger, and to get even."

Autocratic environments display evidence of all three of these motivations. And, studies show that autocratic (dictatorial) climates at home, school, and work produce the following performance expectations:

15% will *achieve.*

70% will exhibit *mediocre* behavior.

15 % will exhibit *rebellious or "get even"* behavior.

On the other hand, a democratic (shared decision making) environment stimulates *achievement* behavior in nearly 100% of any population.

Our spirit or "morale" is either built or destroyed by our surroundings. When morale is high, almost anything is possible. Why does the home team have the advantage in an athletic struggle? Because the crowd is behind them. Hometown support builds morale, which in turn spurs the players to higher performance levels.

I once met an individual who sings opera. He said, "When the audience is with me, I can reach higher notes than I can hit in practice." That morale-inducing, motivational environment inspires him to higher achievement.

Wouldn't it be great if every person had the opportunity to hit the high notes? Just think of the possibilities of a society where there was encouragement at every turn.

Putting Out the Fire

In a country where every person is free to rise to the limits of his or her potential, it should be noted that eighty-five percent of Americans are creative rather than logical thinkers. It's our natural environment and heritage.

Roger Yepsen, Jr, who has done extensive research on the creative personality, says, "Original, mold breaking ideas are more apt to occur in some of us than others. Luckily, any family, company, or country needs to complement its idea-people with implementers, those who can take an idea and put it into action."

Yepsen lists the characteristics used to describe both creative and logical people:

The Idea Person (Creative)

- Flexible, spontaneous, nonjudgmental; unconventional.

- Trusts intuition, does not necessarily proceed from one logical step to another; takes advantage of chance and accident.

- Undisciplined, scattered in attention, not well organized.

- More interested in coming up with ideas than in implementing them.

- Restless with plodding pace of school or job; may not learn necessary skills (consequently, not rewarded with good grades or promotions).

The Implementer (Logical)

- Thorough and dependable.
- Thinks in progression of logical steps; uncomfortable with uncertainty.
- Has the drive and single-mindedness to see the project through.
- Is content to set to work on a less-than brilliant idea; more practical than idealistic.
- Has the technical knowledge needed to get the job done (apt to be rewarded at school or on job).

When we examine the subsystems in our society: the home, the school, and the workplace—it is easy to see why so few people are high achievers. I've met parents who give inflexible rules rather than choices, teachers who force every child to progress at the exact same pace, and supervisors who believe there can be no exceptions to company policy.

Our institutions tend to be authoritative, domineering, and controlled. They cancel the attributes of our political system and immobilize creative thinkers, destroying their willingness to succeed.

Having produced a population of creative thinkers, we promptly place them into environments that seem calculated to extinguish their imagination and turn them into failures.

The fire, reduced to embers, dies.

Analytical, logical people—that fifteen percent—are better suited to succeed in autocratic climates. They actually thrive on it as they move through the ranks to higher positions of authority. Research shows that first-borns usually fall in this category.

Creative thinkers, populated by an extremely high number of later-borns, need an environment of encouragement. They are more likely to succeed in entrepreneurial endeavors where they can put their ideas into action. The organization that capitalizes on their abilities will be the one that offers a democratic, cooperative atmosphere in which they can share in the decision making. That is the direction in which America must be headed in the 21st century.

Here is how it works.

Let me tell you about a woman who had two daughters. The first-born had an excellent record in school, but the younger daughter was having difficulty. The mother asked her older daughter to help her younger sister with her school work. The older child was pleased. It was a recognition of her scholastic proficiency as well as of her status as an older sister. The younger sister made great academic strides because her big sister was no longer a rival she could never beat; she was an ally who could help her to achieve.

How can a parent transform competition into cooperation? Here's one example. Tell all the children that if all their rooms are tidy by a certain time you will take them all out for pizza. It's surprising how quickly those rooms will become neat and clean. You won't have to supervise them and you won't have to tell them to cooperate.

The moment you begin to give those around you an opportunity to participate in activities and decisions, you will be doing yourself, and them, a great favor.

By embarking on a deliberate course involving students in the decision-making process, a high school in Alaska, Mount Edgecumbe, has been able to produce a remarkable student achievement record. The grades of their 200 students improved to nearly 4.0 and "bad conduct" reports were almost totally eliminated.

The rediscovery of democracy at work is the first step on the road to success.

2
The Miracle of Shared Goals

In organized sports, teamwork is viewed as the essential element of success. The legendary Notre Dame coach Knute Rockne said, "The secret of winning football games is working more as a team, less as individuals. I play not my eleven best, but my best eleven."

You can be a great football quarterback, a superb major league baseball pitcher, or a basketball star, but if you depend on your own talent for success, you'll be disappointed. National Hockey League star Wayne Gretzky put it this way: "One guy can't win the Stanley Cup or the Boston Bruins would have won it seven straight years with Bobby Orr. The better the team plays, the better you play."

What is true in sports is also true in the classroom and in the boardroom. When an objective is shared, everybody wins.

David and Roger Johnson, in their book *Circles of Learning*, describe the three choices teachers have in the classroom:

1. Teachers can structure lessons competitively so that students work against each other to achieve a goal that only one or a few students can attain.

2. Teachers can structure lessons individualistically so that students work by themselves to accomplish learning goals unrelated to those of the other students.

3. Teachers can structure lessons cooperatively so that students work together to accomplish shared goals.

The third option offers many advantages. In such a learning environment, "there is a positive interdependence among students' goal attainments; students perceive that they can reach their learning goals if and only if the other students in the learning group also reach their goals."

Research by the Johnsons at the University of Minnesota and in public schools validate the effectiveness of such an approach. Educators are now being trained to employ cooperative learning in the classroom. In many situations it's the last remaining hope.

Interchangeable Parts

Just after World War II, American business turned a deaf ear to the innovative labor-management concepts of an American engineer named W. Edwards Deming. What did he do? Deming took his concepts about the development of workers, training, and team management to Japan. His former critics now credit Deming's ideas as a significant factor in the revival and dominance of Japanese industry. The key to Japan's success was bringing workers into the decision-making process. Business leaders in the United States failed to follow Deming's lead.

> *For too long American executives*
> *have treated workers as interchangeable*
> *parts on an assembly line.*

But that is now changing. In the past decade, broad sweeping changes in management methods, productivity strategies, quality methods, and training techniques have been taking place. These changes were dictated by the realization that education, business, and industry were not keeping pace with international advances in quality and teamwork processes.

Traditional bureaucratic and autocratic management styles are being replaced with supervisory techniques that tend to stimulate human self-value and personal development. Teamwork is appearing with greater frequency at the corporate level.

For example, Richard Wellins and Jill George, associates at Development Dimensions International in Pittsburgh, recently completed a study of SDTs—Self Directed Teams. An SDT is "a small group of employees responsible for an entire work process or segment."

Wellins and George, writing in *Training & Development Journal,* compare SDTs with traditional organizations:

- They're usually leaner, with fewer layers of managers and supervisors.

- The leader is more coach than planner and controller.

- The reward systems tend to be skill- or team- based, rather than seniority-based.

- Information—such as productivity data, quality reports, sales figures, and profit margins—is shared readily with all employees, not just the top few.

- Employees are expected to learn all the jobs and tasks required of the team, not just a single job or task.

Companies such as Microsoft, Boeing, IBM, and Honda of America embrace the team concept because the effort pays off in performance and sales dividends. Significant improvement has been documented in productivity, quality, employee satisfaction, and customer service excellence.

The teams at Honda and those champions in athletics have much in common. Winning isn't produced by solo performances—it's a team effort. As Ray Kroc, the founder of McDonald's said,

A well-run restaurant is like a winning baseball team; it makes the most of every crew member's talent and takes advantage of every split-second opportunity to speed up service.

Listen to the Cook

Jack Eckerd and Charles Colson, in their book *Why American Doesn't Work,* tell the story of candy maker Frank Brock, who hired a team of top engineers to design a new plant after employees complained about the old one.

When the designers showed Brock their plans, he took them to the employees who would be cooking the candy.

"It's a fine-looking building," said one of Brock's best cooks. "But that sugar valve looks like it's about twenty feet away from the steam valve."

"What's wrong with that?" asked Brock.

"Well nothing," smiled the cook, "except that I have to have my hands on both valves at the same time."

As a result of team input, the new plant had an extremely smooth start-up.

Said Eckerd and Colson, "If organizations are to operate effectively, leadership must get into the trenches. Management reports are no match for the personal touch."

Team building, including programs of Quality Processes, Management-Customer Relations, and Management-Employee Relations, have been designated as essential strategies for the future economic health of our nation.

Today, teamwork concepts have emerged as having a most significant effect on the quality of people and products. These same strategies have stimulated interest in the role of the home and educational community in assisting the implementations of these social and managerial innovations. The underlying philosophy can be summarized by the saying: "It is better to have one person working with you than three people working for you."

The Source of Supply

People in every arena of life are coming to the conclusion that we do not live in isolation. There is a well-known idiom in Japan: "to eat from the same pot." It's true. Anyone associated with a business enterprise "eats from the same pot" whether he or she is a shipping clerk, a receptionist, a technician, an accountant, or the company president.

If the pot were to disappear, everyone would go hungry. But when the pot is full, the bounty produced by labor is shared by every worker.

Notable "movers and shakers," including Bill Gates of Microsoft, Charles Schwab of Charles Schwab Corporation, and Herb Kelleher of Southwest Airlines, have continually stressed the theme of teamwork as the key to their corporation's success.

Just this past Spring, Bill Gates said that he, "attributed Microsoft's success to innovation and teamwork." And as you know from the last chapter, a team environment encourages creativity—a key component of innovation.

Historical notable H. Ross Perot of EDS and presidential candidate fame probably said it the best: "Business is not just doing deals; business is having great products, doing great engineering, and providing tremendous service to customers. Finally, business is a cobweb of human relationships."

When all members of an organization see themselves as doing their part, their self-worth is greatly increased. As the mouse said to the elephant as they walked across a bridge, "Together we're shaking this thing."

Many people, however, fail to see the relationship between doing their personal best and being a member of a team. We can learn a lesson from what happened to a textile worker who got caught up in some yarn. He tried and tried to get himself untangled. The more he tried to free himself, the more tangled he became.

Foreman: "Why didn't you call me?"

Worker: "I was trying to do the best I could."

Foreman: "You would have done your best by
           calling me."

We need to realize that we can do our best by working together.

The Basics of Survival

The theme of "shared goals" is driven by ongoing research that supports the notion that competition is a negative found within most human entities. Continuing studies suggest that only fifteen to twenty percent of the population function well in an environment where they are forced to be competitive with others.

To look at it another way, eighty to eighty-five percent of the population seem inhibited about achievement because of the existing business and educational "dog-eat-dog" environments they are in, which are based on internal competition.

For teamwork to work in education, business, and human relationships, there must be a climate that fosters unselfishness and generosity. We can learn a great lesson about such climate from how bees survive through the bitter cold of winter.

Bees live through cold temperatures by a strategy of committing to a common cause and through mutual aid. They form into a ball and keep up what amounts to non-stop motion that resembles a dance.

To accomplish their goal the bees change places; those that have been on the cold outer edge move to the center, and those at the center move out. If those at the center insisted on staying there, keeping the others at the edges, they would all perish.

When goals and objectives are shared the results produce miracles.

> *The key to success—whether*
> *on the sports field, the work*
> *environment, or in the game of*
> *life—is cooperative teamwork.*

> *An eagle*
> *does not fly with just one wing.*
> *It takes two.*

Feelings of "exclusion"—not being on a team or a part of anything worthwhile—are often the source of "mediocre" or "rebellious" performance. In most environments (including schools), individuals are subjectively excluded from any team or positive identity.

At the Plainfield (Indiana) Middle School, however, any-one who wants to be a cheerleader, member of a sports team, band member, or a part of any "positive identity" activity is "on the team." And there is another rule—"no cuts." However, to maintain team status, students must show up for practices and scheduled activities to learn what is necessary to perform effectively.

What has been the result? The morale, productivity and academic performance of the students at Plainfield is extremely high. Plus, there is a tremendous involvement on the part of the parents. They are considered part of the "team."

The program, in which half the students are involved in extracurricular activities (compared with 20% nationwide), was recently featured on CNN, ABC, and NBC news.

Here is the bottom line: *You can't successfully compete externally if you compete internally.* When people are in a contest with each other, everybody loses. When they cooperate, everybody wins.

3
Beyond Competition

Is there hope for the long-neglected creative person in our educational and business environment? I am happy to report that there is promise, and it's accomplished by the team approach.

An elementary school in Indianapolis has been pioneering a way to develop children by teaching them to use all seven of their innate intelligences. Harvard psychologist Howard Gardner, in his book *Frames of Mind: The Theory of Multiple Intelligences*, lists them as:

1. **Linguistic:** Our facility with language
2. **Logical-mathematical:** The ability to recognize patterns and order
3. **Spatial:** The capacity to visualize material things
4. **Bodily-kinesthetic:** The ability to make the mind and body work together
5. **Interpersonal:** The facility to observe and make distinctions among others; the ability to read people
6. **Intrapersonal:** The ability to look into one's self and understand what one sees; an introspective ability to understand what drives ones own behavior
7. **Musical:** A sensitivity to pitch, melody, tone, and rhythm

The Indianapolis educators developed a series of games designed to challenge each of the intelligences. By observing childrens' performances, they could identify the areas in which they excelled.

Having determined this, they organized the classroom into teams of seven, each member excelling in a different intelligence.

Instead of grading individuals, the teachers graded the teams.

After one year, all students in the study had high measurable skills in all seven intelligences. The studies have been replicated in high school, with the same results.

Here's what happened: In the team environment, the person excelling in the particular field being studied would help fellow team members master it. When they were studying math, the logical child would naturally take the lead. When they were studying music, the child with the musical intelligence would take over. On the playground, the one with the physical intelligence would help teammates master body skills.

This spirit of cooperation generated an excitement unseen in the old competitive system.

The beauty of the cooperative approach is that the creative person learns without holding back the logical thinker since both logical and creative thinkers thrive in a democratic, cooperative environment. But in an autocratic, competitive arena only the logical thinker can hack it.

There's an added benefit, because in such an environment the creative child learns the logical skills needed to break through to achievement.

The democratic, cooperative environment tends to eliminate the extremes. A logical-thinking student, accustomed to leadership, will still excel. But the creative-thinking child will not be left out in the cold.

Rewriting the Manual

The same principle of teamwork produces amazing results in business.

In a Rockwell plant in Ohio the manager spent the majority of his time making sure the morale of his workers was at least seven on a scale of one to ten. He welcomed their ideas and often put them into practice. The plant has a huge press that stamps out axle halves for heavy-duty trucks. Periodically, the plant had to close a shift while the press was retooled. The plant engineers had written a "change manual" to guide the hourly workers in the retooling process.

One day, the employees went to the manager. "If we follow the engineers' manual," they said, "it takes twelve hours to do the retooling. If you give us a chance, we think we can save you some time."

He was listening to men and women with high school educations—or less. The manager could have thought,

*Why should I pay attention
to workers who are second-guessing
engineering graduates from
major universities?*

In most plants, the rule is: Engineers write the manuals; hourly workers follow them.

But this manager was different. "Why don't you come to my office and let's discuss it," he said.

As a result of this discussion, these creative workers came up with an idea that could be implemented with the help of some special tooling. When the requested devices were made, instead of taking hours to retool, it took just under fifteen minutes. When you realize that in some manufacturing environments it costs up to $10,000 an hour to shut down an operation, it's not hard to conclude that those creative employees saved Rockwell a bundle.

What happened in that plant?

The employees were functioning in a democratic, cooperative environment. They adopted the goals and principles of the company as their own. Their job was not just to run a press; it was to make money for their company, to protect jobs, and to maintain a competitive plant.

Time for a Bonus

Creative people, when they become achievers, tend to become entrepreneurs.

That doesn't always mean that they have to go into business for themselves. Large companies can turn ingenious employees into contributors by giving them a piece of the decision-making action. Instead of trying to control them, the company gives employees a chance at control. The results of what happened at the Rockwell axle-making plant speak for themselves.

At a foundry in Elyria, Ohio, Gregg Foster knew the business he was about to buy was in deep trouble. "Basically, the company was in free fall. The numbers were bleak, the trends were scary, and I didn't have answers. The foundry was losing three million dollars a year."

Foster began the turnaround by first shutting the company down for three days and interviewing three hundred "former" employees for possible rehire. They hired the one hundred candidates with the best performance and attendance records.

He gathered the rehired workforce and said, "I don't care what you used to do—it didn't work. As of last Friday, this became a new company, and we're doing things differently." And he announced, "I intend to share profits with everyone here."

> *Foster saved his company by introducing team concepts. In return, he got a supportive workforce and harmonious labor relations.*

Foster got rid of six company cars, canceled company memberships at three country clubs, and established an atmosphere of management-labor unity. Productivity increased dramatically. Instead of 391 employees producing twelve thousand tons of castings annually, a few years later the same output was achieved with only 216 workers. He personally set the tone for the company's dramatic growth.

In the first eight years of his leadership only three employees left the foundry, an unheard-of turnover rate. Not incidentally, his foundry survived as a profitable operation while many others around him faced financial jeopardy.

The Open Door

In Bay City, Michigan, Patricia Carrigan became the manager of the General Motors plant. She earned an enviable reputation for being adept at walking into situations of labor-management polarization and calming the atmosphere. She did it by just showing up.

One of the first things Carrigan did at the Bay City plant

was to personally meet every one of her 2,300 workers. She looked each one in the eye and shook their hands. "People want to be recognized as people," she says.

Carrigan acquired her management wisdom while teaching third grade in public schools. It was in the classroom that she made a simple but insightful discovery:

> *When people were happy, learning was easy;*
> *when people were unhappy,*
> *learning was difficult.*

It works in the classroom; it works on the factory floor.

One of the things Carrigan did was to set an example by leaving her office door open. She encouraged other managers to do the same. Management was no longer inaccessible to employees. If you wanted to see Pat, you walked right in. That is, if she was there. Most of the time you would find her out on the floor, talking to the employees, getting to know them, listening to their ideas.

Patricia Carrigan was at the cutting edge of management philosophy for the 21st century. The companies that survive to compete in the next century will be the companies that foster democratic, cooperative, morale—inducing environments. These new business climates will enable them to tap into the enormous creative resources of the American population.

Capacity for Change

You may wonder what happens to those noncooperative thinkers when management asks them to become part of the decision-making team. The answer is that they become active participants. It won't happen overnight. You can't keep people on a payroll for twenty years without asking their opinions, and then expect them to become a fountain of ideas overnight.

In time, however, workers change. How long it takes depends upon the degree of autocratic control they experienced in the old environment. The range is from one to six years. But eventually, the noncooperative thinkers learn to think for themselves, for the company, and for their future.

An automobile plant in Cincinnati committed to a system of total employee involvement. Of the twenty-five hundred workers in that plant, only twenty-five couldn't make the transition. So ninety-nine percent of the people are capable of moving from a controlled, autocratic environment into an entrepreneurial, democratic one.

That's good news, because the creative intellects the people whose talents have been overlooked in the home and in the school—represent the hope of our country for years to come.

Following his retirement as Chairman from Chrysler Motors, Lee Iocca assumed a national prominence in promoting a national attention to education. He was well known for his passion for educational excellence for "all students" (not just the chosen few) and was able to bring education into the national spotlight. He made the timeless observation that "the future does not depend upon what our top students can do; it depends upon what our average students can do."

There are millions of "average" students and workers waiting to be challenged. When people in routine jobs become entrepreneurial, the change stimulates them to become fully-functioning intellectual, physiological human beings.

Your New Environment

Perhaps you are beginning to understand why I am so pas-
sionate about changing the autocratic arena of home, school,
and workplace into a democratic, cooperative environment.
It is the only way we will be able to survive in the future.

> *When we stop competing with*
> *each other, we start competing*
> *with the world. And that will be good*
> *for America and foreign nations.*

Perhaps you have said, "I'm a creative person and I don't
think I stand a chance in the highly structured or autocratic
climate of my company."

The good news is that your environment is in the process
of change. The enterprises that are going to survive will be
democratic, cooperative companies that view their employees as a team and as a corporate asset.

While cooperation is a unique process to bring people
together to complete a common goal, cooperation can be
expanded beyond a company or organization.

Here is a case in point. *Forbes* magazine recently reported
on how Honda of America Manufacturing fosters a team
relationship with suppliers using a "comangement" approach.
While many companies are using offshore suppliers to mini-
mize costs, Honda works directly with a Michigan supplier
teaching them how to do better with their existing operation.
With process changes and machinery upgrades the supplier
company was able to compete with foreign suppliers' cost
structure and retain its supplier relationship with Honda.
This cooperative relationship saved an American supplier,
not to mention the jobs and the local economy. Honda was

so pleased with the result that it has added two additional companies to its comanagement program. Says Timothy Myers at Honda,

> *We took the long view*
> *that by working together,*
> *we could make them competitive.*

Now that's cooperation. That's teamwork. That's success!

Here's more good news. If the working conditions at your place of employment are not changing, plenty of other environments are. And as a creative person, you have unlimited opportunities in the marketplace once you recognize the potential within yourself.

Take a self-inventory.

- In which of the seven intelligences do you excel?
- What are the possibilities of exploiting and promoting those talents?
- Are there enterprises that will give you the chance to share your talents in a participative way?
- What opportunities can you see for using your abilities in a venture of your own?

When a *Business Week* report graded the ability of Harvard University's School of Business to develop leadership in students, the prestigious school was given high marks in most categories except for the area of "teamwork." Why? Two of the reasons were that a "forced grading curve discourages cooperation" and "courses require very little group work."

Since then, recommendations were made not only for Harvard, but for all business schools to place emphasis on group processes and team decision making. The majority (if not all) of America's business schools and particularly the graduate MBA programs have placed a focus on team processes and using group practices for most of the course work.

There is no substitute for cooperative effort.

You don't have to excel in every area to be a success. If there is a gap in your skills, you can join forces with others to add even greater strength. When you form a team, watch how the power multiplies.

4
The "Inside" Team

I remember the day I spoke to a group of high school students in Illinois, who were classified as learning-disadvantaged. At one point, I asked them why they were in that class.

"I guess it's because we're stupid," one of them answered.

The rest of the class cheered and I realized it was now up to me to convince them that they were not stupid.

I began asking them a few questions. I wondered how many of them were intuitive. They didn't know what that meant.

"How many of you believe nobody can put anything over on you?" Everyone's hand went up.

"How many of you like music and believe you have a talent for it?"

Almost everyone raised a hand.

"How many of you are pretty good at sports?"

Again, hands went up all over the room.

"How many of you feel like you know yourselves well?"

"I didn't before but I think I'm starting to today," one boy answered.

I went down the list of Gardner's seven intelligences (listed in chapter three), and I found these young people proficient in at least five of them. They happened to be deficient in the one for which they were tested—the logical intelligence. Because of this, the one hundred and fifty creative young people in that room were judged to be "suspect" learners.

The sad part is that they had bought into the fallacy and were behaving accordingly.

All the children in the group were gifted in several areas. And I encouraged them to begin to build on their strengths. "If you're musical, team up with someone who is good at writing," I told them. "There's no telling what you can produce."

The students left with something they hadn't brought with them—self-confidence in their abilities.

Brain Power

I believe that personal esteem and high morale are essential to achievement. I've seen it over and over; when your spirits are lifted you become naturally creative. But when morale is low, as found in an atmosphere of punitive discipline, hopelessness prevails. There is another important factor.

People in habitually low-morale environments end up destroying their own self-esteem. They feel they are worthless.

That is why the teenagers in Illinois believed the people who told them they were stupid.

Why does this happen? Research into the human brain provides some of the answers.

The thing that distinguishes the human brain from the animal brain is the cerebral cortex, a thick layer of gray matter at the outer regions of the brain. That's where the source of our creative and reasoning abilities are housed.

Research by brain specialist Marian Diamond found that when our spirits are low, day in and day out, the cerebral cortex actually becomes thin. But when our morale is continually up, the cerebral cortex thickens. In other words, morale affects the size of your brain, *the important* part of your brain, where you think and create.

Morale is affected by the type of environment in which you find yourself. If you are a creative thinker, you have a low tolerance for boredom and need constant excitement to keep your attitude positive. That does not happen in rigid, autocratic environments—the kind you find in most classrooms and workplaces. You get bored and "turned off." Both your morale and your creativity are diminished.

People who are analytical in nature don't have this problem. They can actually adapt to a boring environment. They don't need constant stimulation. What is their secret?

Little Jolts of Euphoria

Science tells us that such people have an abundant supply of something called "beta endorphins," that give them the equivalent of a perpetual high. It's like a support team working inside your body. Unfortunately, if you are a creative thinker, you don't have an abundance of that resource.

What are beta endorphins, and how did you come up shortchanged?

The answer goes back to your childhood.

Beta endorphins are little jolts
of pain-killing and euphoria-producing
chemicals generated in various
parts of your brain.

Your brain has a set of receptors for beta endorphins. When the jolt hits, these receptors respond by killing pain and rewarding you with a magnificent euphoria. The jolts can become addictive.

Exercise can stimulate the generation of beta endorphins. That may explain why people can get hooked on running: They'll jog through rain, through snow, and through Central Park to get their endorphin highs.

For many people, endorphins are linked to what is known as "runner's high"—a unique feeling of wellbeing that comes after an aerobic workout.

We have all heard the stories of marathon runners who finish a race hardly noticing serious injuries, including stress fractures, that may have happened along the way. The next day, when they are in a leg cast, they'll say, "I really didn't feel the pain."

The Cuddle Cure

How do we get beta endorphins without harming ourself?

You developed your capacity for generating beta endorphins on your mother's lap. A child loves the warmth and security of an adult's presence, and when a child snuggles comfortably in a parental lap, the beta-endorphin pumps start throbbing. The child receives a pleasant high while nestling there.

When your own child comes to your room in the middle of the night and wants to climb in bed with you, don't turn the child away. Your offspring is looking for a "high" and your very presence stimulates the secretion of beta endorphins. That is why when you're with someone you love you feel at ease and secure. But when you're separated, you feel depressed.

A child that is held and cuddled
day in and day out develops a powerful system for
secreting beta endorphins.

This capacity remains throughout life. If you received ample doses of beta endorphins as a child, through affection, your system still pumps them out, and you don't need extraordinary excitement to keep your morale up.

Dr. Bernie Siegel, in his book *Love, Medicine and Miracles,* says, "If we weren't hugged enough as children or loved unconditionally, that is, just for ourselves, rather than for being neat, smart, polite, obedient—a "good" girl or boy—we might not feel worthwhile as adults either, making ourselves vulnerable to illness."

If you were denied your quota of cuddling and hugging during childhood, then your beta endorphin pump never developed to its fullest capacity. It needs constant priming. You need excitement and stimulation to keep your morale up. Siegel says it is important that we learn to love ourselves, to replace what might have been lost.

Perhaps you are beginning to understand why the supportive home environment tends to produce logical thinkers while the nonsupportive environment produces creative thinkers.

This should not be taken as an indictment of the parents of eighty-five percent of the American people. It is a recognition of a natural tendency: Parents normally lavish more attention on firstborns and, in some cases, lastborns; the middle child gets less attention. And middle children almost inevitably finish second to older siblings in physical and mental feats during early childhood.

If you're a parent, make sure the middle youngsters get their share of warm hugs and praise. Teach the importance of cooperation and make sure their achievements get equal billing with the achievements of their siblings.

The Vicious Spiral

Creative thinkers need morale-inducing environments to stimulate their creativity. If they don't find them, their brains run short of beta endorphins, their morale plunges, and their cerebral cortex shrinks. As a result, their creative ability is diminished, their self-esteem plummets, and their morale drops even further. It becomes a vicious spiral.

This is what typically happens when creative people emerge from nonsupportive home environments and enter autocratic classrooms. They go in with a scant stash of beta endorphins. They are asked to compete, but competition is deadly to their morale, which consequently drops. Performance stays low.

Later, when they enter the work environment, the outcome is predictable. If it's an autocratic environment, the process is repeated.

> *Most creative thinkers are branded as non-achievers and they continue in their cycles of mediocre performance.*

This is what happened to the kids in Illinois. The autocratic school environment had already branded them as "slow" and destroyed their morale. Without knowing it, the school system was creating a climate of negative growth.

Donna's Braids

I once asked my wife, "Who has been the greatest influence on your life?" I waited for the expected response: How could she be married to me and not be uplifted by my superbly-honed motivational skills?

I wasn't prepared for her answer. The big influence on her life had been Miss Vigrant, her third-grade teacher.

"And what marvelous motivational technique did Miss Vigrant use?" I wanted to know.

Donna had been an indifferent student who gravitated toward the back of the room and tuned everyone out.

One day Miss Vigrant came over to her and said, "Donna, you have lovely hair. Why don't you ask your mother to put it up in pigtails?"

Donna passed on the suggestion to her mother. The next day, Donna went to school with her hair in braids. Miss Vigrant noticed. She told her how pretty she looked. Later in the day, one of the braids came undone.

"Donna, would you stay a little while after school?" said Miss Vigrant. After school, the teacher patiently rebraided the hair.

Soon after that episode, Donna began gravitating toward the front of the room. She became interested in everything Miss Vigrant taught.

She stayed in touch with her third-grade teacher throughout school and throughout life, writing her regularly to let her know where she was and what she was doing. She had found a good, reliable source of beta endorphins.

Donna's new perspective on herself and her abilities led to improved school work, and from this came many life and career gains.

You can also cultivate sources of beta endorphins beyond the circle of family and school. Everyone needs a support group. By that, I don't mean a group of troubled people gathering in the office of a psychiatrist, who puffs benignly on a pipe and keeps repeating, in a carefully neutral voice, I hear you saying that you need more beta endorphins…

What you need is a circle of
positive friends with whom you
can relax, have a few laughs, share
friendly conversation, and
enjoy mutual respect.

A bowling league may be a source of beta endorphins. Or you may find stimulation in service organizations or social clubs. Can you take on a Scout troop? How about volunteering for rescue-squad duty? Does your community have a volunteer fire department? Can you help out at the hospital or a local anti-poverty agency?

These activities may seem to have little bearing on your vocational success. But they can give you a sense of self-worth and self-confidence. They can also raise your morale—the prerequisite for achievement.

The encouragement from your team transforms you from the inside out.

5
We're In This Thing Together

"There's an error on this blueprint," I told a fellow employee. "What should I do?"

"Build it exactly like the guy drew it," was his reply.

I was a young man, about twenty-three years old. My training at General Motors was finished and this was my first "solo" job as a tool-and-die maker. A man from the front office—in his white shirt, suit and tie—brought me the blueprints and I started working on building the metal stamping device called the die.

About halfway through the project I realized there was an error on the blueprint. It was then I turned to a fellow worker for advice. His answer to "build it like the guy drew it" surprised me.

My heart began to sink. I didn't want to build a die that would break. But the guys on the floor encouraged me. The next day it seemed that dozens of men came to my bench, patting me on the back and trying to make me a hero because I was going to make an engineer look bad.

Occasionally, believe it or not, the engineers made mistakes. Usually, believe it or not, the tool-and-die makers *caught* those mistakes. What was their response? Did they walk to the engineering office and point out the error in order to save the company time and money? Guess again.

*What I was encouraged to do was
to make a white collar "genius"
look bad. It's called "malicious
obedience"—a defensive tactic that
results from destroyed morale.*

It is a great barrier to productivity in the American work place.

When faced with the dilemma of making a die that wouldn't work, I couldn't bring myself to do it. Instead, I covertly made the corrections so I could live with my own conscience.

Let's Figure This Out

Six months later, another engineer came to my bench. He didn't have a blueprint. Instead, he had a little prototype part—a model of what the eventual part would look like when it was mass-produced.

"Charles," he said, "I want you to look at this. I'm responsible for designing the die. Let's see if we can sit down and figure out a different way to do it."

That engineer was on to something. Almost from the moment he walked into my environment he turned me into a creative, concept-generating person. I gave him ideas I would never have dreamed of before that meeting. Why? He treated me as an equal. He raised my morale and self-worth. And when morale is raised, creativity is stimulated.

Three weeks later he brought me the blueprints and I began making the die. In the process, sure enough, I found a mistake. Immediately I called him and said, "We have made a mistake."

It wasn't me, and it wasn't him. He said, "I'm sure we can solve the problem. After all, we're in this thing together."

What had the engineer done? He had transformed the environment, from an authoritarian arena that was murder on morale, into a cooperative atmosphere that was both stimulating and refreshing.

As much as we wish for it, there will never be a time that we are totally surrounded by team players. In fact, there are usually more "vultures" flying around than we would like to admit.

When I speak to young people I mention that of all our acquaintances, only a fourth of them like us "warts and all." They become part of the supporting team. About another fourth either dislike you or don't want to be in your company. The remaining fifty percent are undecided. Your success often depends on how you allow these groups to influence you.

Young people find it hard to accept the fact that one out of four people who know them dislikes them. It's hard to handle rejection.

Youth and adults often find themselves in environments where young people and older adults interact. Those environments could be in schools, workplaces, or social situations. Often, adults overly impressed with their own importance look down their noses at young people who don't fit the "proper" mold. Without saying it, their subtle behavior communicates, "you're beneath my dignity. You'll never come up to my standard."

Those kinds of signals can destroy young people. It may cause them to develop defensive personalities, indulge in the thrill of insubordination, and eventually become addicted to negative thinking and behavior.

Young and Quick?

What should we do with people who are not on our team? Should we run and hide? Should we mirror their behavior and seek to harm them? Never! Instead, we should consciously allow their actions to "spur" our achievement.

It has often been said, "Don't become bitter, become better."

Paul Harvey tells the story of a woman who didn't know the value of teamwork.

He told of a Dallas woman who drove her Mercedes Benz around a crowded parking lot, looking for a space to park in. Finally, she saw a man placing his purchases in the trunk of his car. She stopped and waited patiently for him to leave the space.

The man backed out and drove away. But before the woman could pull in, a young man in a silver Corvette whipped in ahead of her.

"Young man," she said, controlling her anger, "It must have been obvious to you that I was waiting quite a while for that space. Why did you pull in ahead of me?"

The cocky youth answered, "Because I'm young and I'm quick."

The woman's morale was completely destroyed and she took defensive action. She backed her Mercedes around, fastened her seat belt, then jerked it into drive and floored the accelerator. She rear-ended the Corvette and totaled both cars.

"Why on earth did you do that?" asked the distraught young man whose snazzy sports car had become a piece of junk.

"Because," she replied, "I am old and I'm very rich."

Harvey swears the story is true.

We don't need to become confrontational with people, but on the other hand, don't expect everyone to give you smiles and hugs along your journey.

The Wish for Failure

If you think that when you strike out on your own, your acquaintances will cheer you on, think again. Even when you succeed, don't expect everyone to applaud. It won't happen.

I remember the time that two school teachers in our community sold everything they owned, bought some equipment, and began mining coal on leased land in Kentucky.

Did their colleagues send them off to the beat of a marching band and the sound of popping champagne corks? No. Their fellow employees secretly wanted them to fail. Why? Because the two teachers were taking risks their colleagues were unwilling to take.

Their fellow teachers wanted their own cautious judgments to be vindicated.

If your enterprise becomes wildly successful, don't expect that to change their minds either. Your acquaintances will envy you because you're doing something they wish they had the courage to do. Envy is truly a green-eyed monster.

You can take comfort in the fact that twenty-five percent of your acquaintances will like you regardless—rich or poor, successful or unsuccessful.

These are the people you need to cultivate in the building of your team. But don't despise the critics. Use their arrows to prod you on.

The Plastic Cow

The vultures can motivate you, as they did in the case of Stew Leonard, in Norwalk, Connecticut.

Stew opened a dairy business, delivering milk door to door. That was contrary to all logic.

"You'll never make it, Stew!" cried the critics. "Everybody buys milk from the supermarkets these days." Then they sat back on their perches, waiting to feast their psyches on Stew's failure.

From the start of his enterprise, Stew was inventive. He figured that people like a little variety in their lives. So he mounted a plastic cow atop his delivery truck, and hung a bell around her neck. Wherever Stew went, people recognized the plastic cow and the sound of her bell.

Stew's merchandising was an immediate success. When he had milked the plastic-cow gimmick for all it was worth, he applied the same kind of intuition to a dairy store he opened. The first year of the operation he barely broke even. The vultures chortled and wagged their heads. "By next year," they thought, "Leonard's business would surely be a corpse."

Some corpse! Within a few years, Stew Leonard's thriving operation had grossed about seventy million dollars, compared to a typical grocery store that grosses seven million. Stew was heralded by some as "the world's most successful retailer." Corporations were loading their jets and taking their entire staff to Norwalk to see his operation.

In 2007, *Fortune* magazine's "100 Best Companies to Work For" article rated Stew Leonard's store at number 51.

What Stew did was to build upon a central concept that people want novelty in their lives. He also devised a way to make every customer a member of his team. He accomplished it with his shopping bag that has become world famous.

If you take a picture of yourself with the bag, Stew will pay you three dollars and post it on a special display board in the store. He has a picture of a couple standing on the Great Wall of China, holding a Stew Leonard shopping bag. There's a snapshot of a scuba-diving couple in the Bahamas—their shopping bag clearly visible through the blue waters of the Caribbean.

Another way Leonard turns his customers into team members is to encourage them to make suggestions for improvements or to recommend products they would like to see added. There are so many ideas submitted that the box has to be emptied twice a day.

One suggestion came from a woman who didn't want other people picking out her strawberries. So Stew established a special counter where people could pick out their own strawberries and put them in quart-size plastic containers.

The result: the customer who comes in to buy a quart of strawberries gets carried away and ends up picking out several quarts.

He uses many techniques to build his team. Each month Stew puts twelve new people on an advisory board to give their personal input on how he should do business. They are people selected from among his customers.

A three-ton "Rock of Commitment" is used to display the rules of the store. They include: "(1) The customer is always right, and (2) If the customer is ever wrong, reread Rule One."

There is another sign Stew hangs in his dairy: "If you

wouldn't take it home to your mother, don't put it out for our customers."

I offer Stew Leonard as a role model, with one caveat:

> *Before embarking on your own enterprise, get competent counsel. If you don't know what you're doing, find somebody who does and ask for advice.*

You should always consider advice from "non-doers" as suspicious.

Ready to Join Forces

When you try to operate on your own, the going can be slow. Let me give an example.

I happen to own a small private airplane and when I bought it I needed a place to park it. I found a small hangar for sale and spent four months trying to gather information on how much the property was worth. I admit that I know very little about real estate values. Finally, I went to a trusted friend who is a banker. Within thirty minutes, he was able to give me a reliable figure on what I should be paying for the hangar.

There are people everywhere who are willing to be supportive. Most of them will offer their help if you will just ask. There will always be that twenty-five percent who have their noses in the air. But the vast majority are ready to join forces if you'll just give them the opportunity.

You will smile when you hear them say, "I'm glad to help. We're in this thing together."

6
The Secret Strategy

The moment you make the transition from an autocratic to a democratic environment—whether it be in education or as an entrepreneur—you have introduced a brand new element into the game plan. It's called *stress.*

You say, "Charles, wait just a minute. I thought dealing with an authoritarian was trouble enough. Why should I turn to a strategy that will produce tension?"

First, let me say that what you experience working for an inflexible authority figure is not so much anxiety as it is fear. In most cases, the fear is eventually replaced by an "I don't care" attitude that usually reduces stress and productivity at the same time.

> ### *When you choose the team approach you are deliberately bringing stress—the good kind—into people's lives.*

Until you get used to being involved and participating in decisions, it is initially stressful.

"Mary, what do you think about the idea?" or

"Bill, how should we solve the problem?"

For perhaps the first time, people are being asked to make independent judgments. It's known as "going out on a limb." Is it stressful? Yes. But from that tension comes creative ideas, and a healthy work environment.

Too Relaxed

A few years ago, the state of Ohio lost a valued manufacturing company. The factory work was shifted to another state, which offered a number of inducements, including major tax breaks, to persuade industries to relocate there.

The problem was that people in this particular section of the state where the company relocated had a lifestyle that was extremely "laid back" and relaxed. They would draw their paychecks on Friday, grab a sixpack on the way home, and prepare for a leisurely weekend. As one person told me, "They got so relaxed they wouldn't show up for work again until Wednesday."

Stress? They didn't have the slightest idea what the word meant.

The managers knew they couldn't stay in the manufacturing business if they continued in such an atmosphere. They returned to rural Ohio, where they found people motivated by a form of self-induced healthy stress known as the "work ethic."

These are the kind of workers who respond positively to strong management and leadership.

You'll find that same ethic all over the country: In Atlanta, in Austin, in Toledo, in Tulsa, in Saginaw, in Seattle, and in vibrant communities across the land. It just happened that this particular company had been directed toward a relaxed, easy-going area where people had not yet learned to use stress to propel them to higher levels of achievement.

A Valued Asset

As a public speaker I have addressed hundreds of audiences. A friend recently said, "Charles, I guess you've given so many talks that you never get nervous anymore. "

"Far from it," I told him. "I'm *always* uptight just before being introduced."

You see, if the adrenalin is not flowing, and I am not "on edge" about the event, I would probably be a failure on the platform. People would say, "He doesn't seem to care about us." Or, "He sure has a cocky attitude."

I consider stress to be one of my most valued assets—*my secret strategy.*

If you want to become a great team player, the same principle applies. As I told someone, "You need to turn yourself into a slingshot."

If you were a creative kid back in the old days before the age of video games and other high-tech toys—you might have amused yourself by making slingshots.

You'd find a sturdy but slender limb with a nice Y-shaped fork, and trim it until the stem of the Y fit comfortably in the hand. You would cut an old inner tube (this was before tubeless tires) into strips of rubber. Then you'd attach a strip to each prong of the "Y." Next, you would punch holes in each end of an old leather shoe tongue and through these holes you'd attach the dangling thongs of rubber.

The shoe tongue would hang like a swing from the "Y." You'd put a rock in that "swing," and be ready to go bird hunting.

But what did it take to propel that rock? Tension, which is a result of stress being applied to the rubber. You'd have to stretch those rubber stirrups until they were trembling with stored energy. Then, when you released the rock, it flew with a velocity that was lethal.

Just as tension-producing stress was required to send the rock on its way, the same thing is required to make your actions effective. Triumph doesn't come from simply forming a team. Success is a team *effort.*

It's Healthy!

Stress gets a bum rap in our society. It has become stigma-tized as the villain in ulcers, heart attacks, strokes, and other illnesses.

> *Medical research has proven that stress—the right kind—is healthy. It becomes positive the moment the mind perceives that what you're doing has a worthy purpose.*

On the other hand, there are countless forms of stress that threaten our well-being. For example, if we are constantly put down in public, our self-value is lowered.

As humans we are meant to be challenged, not to be led like mindless robots. If all hurdles were to be removed from life, your mind would conclude that there was no longer a reason for you to be alive. It would begin shutting down life-sustaining mechanisms. The first thing to go would be the immune system, then your muscles, and finally, the brain it-self. When you are challenged, however, every part of your body strives to make an exciting contribution.

Tension is an important part of a normal functioning body. It is an inner drive that is basic to success. Without it we would be like many psychotics and schizophrenics who seem to live in another world of complete tranquility.

Physician Harry Johnson, chairman of the medical board of the Life Extension Institute, says:

> *For some reason, there seems to be a popular notion that tension is*

> *bad. This isn't so. Like so many other things in life, tension is only harmful in large doses.*

Says Johnson, "A watch spring, for example, cannot perform its function without being under constant tension, but we all know the results of over-winding the watch. It is the same with the human body. Tension that keeps us interested and alert is good and necessary. When we move over the fine borderline where we become apprehensive and anxious and fearful, only then it is bad."

Stress-Resistant

More than likely you have met people who have faced dreadful tragedies in their life. When you hear their stories there is usually one common theme. They'll tell you, "I not only survived, but I learned some great lessons from the crisis."

A "stress-resistant" personality may be their secret weapon, according to Dr. Raymond Flannery, Jr., professor of psychology at Harvard Medical School and author of *Becoming Stress-Resistant.*

For twelve years Flannery studied more than twelve hundred men and women who prevailed over great stress. There were six qualities these people had in common:

- **Personal control.** "The stress-resistant take reasonable charge of the daily hassles that befall them," says Flannery.

- **Task involvement.** Effective "copers" are committed to something important—a career, their children, a volunteer program.

- **Lifestyle choices.** Resilient people have a balanced

diet, exercise at least three times a week, and relax.

- **Humor.** Joking and laughing, and the relaxation it brings, can help people under stress keep life in perspective.
- **Religious beliefs.** "People who have a rich spiritual life have better health and less stress."
- **Social support.** "Adaptive individuals seek the physical and emotional benefits from being with others who provide companionship, information, and help," says Flannery.

The study showed that people who survive great pressures rely on more than their own resources; they have the support of a team.

> *There is no need to burden*
> *yourself with unnecessary pressure*
> *when there are others who*
> *should be sharing the load.*

We need to develop the attitude of the president of a company in Pennsylvania. He was on a golfing vacation when his office manager telephoned. He returned the call from the clubhouse at the end of the ninth hole.

The president listened carefully as the subordinate explained the sticky situation. Then he asked one question: "Are the others worrying?"

"They most certainly are," said the concerned manager.

In a relaxed tone, the president said, "That's fine. If they're worrying, then I can go back to my golf. I will be in the office next week, and then I'll worry while they play."

Life in the Sewer

During World War II, the saga of the French Underground was one of the most remarkable stories of the conflict. These people lived in the filthy sewers of Paris—that's why they called them the Underground. Conditions were rotten. They ate whatever food the above-ground resistance could give them. They banded together, living in the constant knowledge that if they were caught they would be shot immediately.

You would think that in such squalid surroundings with bad food and constant danger, these people would be disease-ridden bundles of nerves.

The fact is that in over four years of underground activity, these survivors rarely even suffered from the common cold. It is said that their immune systems were so powerful that infections didn't stand a chance. Their minds were focused on one thing: survival for themselves, and survival for their friends.

You don't have to live in a sewer and face death daily to be challenged. When you encounter stress it can be life *preserving* if your mind perceives a worthwhile purpose, totally focused on a clear objective. You will find even greater strength in a team environment.

Find a Challenge

As you move toward your goal of success, remember that it isn't responsibility that kills you; it is the feeling that you're not accomplishing anything. You age much, much faster when you're spinning your wheels.

When people retire to a calm, stress-free environment, before long they're totally relaxed—in a coffin. A recent report said that the average life expectancy after retirement for people who don't take on another challenge is only three years.

Remember: It is not stress that keeps you from achieving. It's the absence of challenge.

If you find yourself in a boring rut, unchallenged by your job but content to drift along rather than compete for higher prizes, it's time to put some healthy stress into your life.

You do it by accepting a challenge that will stretch your talents. You also do it by becoming responsible to a group of people who depend on your contribution to their success.

Does the very prospect make you nervous? Good! That tension will give you the drive to flourish and prosper.

It's time to see the big picture. As George Bernard Shaw wrote in *Man and Superman,* "This is the true joy of life, the being used for a purpose recognized by yourself as a mighty one…being a force of nature instead of a feverish, selfish little clod of ailments and grievances complaining that the world will not devote itself to making you happy."

Find yourself a mighty purpose, and let the slingshot of stress propel you toward its fulfillment. It's your secret strategy of success.

7
Say "We!"

"They love me out there," the organist said to the little man who was backstage manually pumping air through the bellows while the concert was being presented.

At the turn of the century it was a popular form of entertainment to attend a pipe organ concert featuring nationally known performers. This was before the invention of the electric organ. While the organist gave his performance, a hired hand would be behind the curtains pumping away for all he was worth. Without his "sweat power," the bellows could not produce a sound.

In Philadelphia, after a concert master had given an outstanding performance, the audience gave the organist a standing ovation as he finished his last number before intermission.

After taking his bows, he rushed back behind the curtain and spoke to the little man who had been pumping the air into the bellows with both his feet. "They love me out there," said the organist.

"What do you mean?" responded the man who had pumped and pumped until he was nearly exhausted. "They love we out there. After all, without me you wouldn't be having a concert."

The organist was indignant. "No," he said, with his nose in the air, they love me. They know talent when they hear it!"

Following the intermission, the organist strutted to the instrument, seated himself, and prepared for an even greater second-half performance. He lifted his arms, and after a dramatic pause his hands came down on the keys.

Nothing happened!

He paused for a moment and tried it once again. Still no sound came from the mighty instrument. After the third embarrassing attempt, he looked around the organ to the corner of the stage. There he saw the "pumper" with his head sticking out of the side of the curtain. The fellow was smiling.

"Say we!" said the little man. "Say *we!*"

We the People

What happened on that concert stage is a lesson that must be learned and re-learned again and again. It is virtually impossible to become a master of anything all alone.

- The CEO of Ford Motor Company would eventually face failure without the support of everyone from managers and foremen to assembly-line workers.

- The best all-pro quarterback cannot win the Super Bowl by himself. He is totally dependent on the team.

- A great film star depends on hundreds of people, from script writers to make-up artists, for success.

- Four-star military generals may wear all the ribbons, but they are in debt to hundreds of courageous men and women.

The list goes on and on.

What about the success of our nation? Can we depend on a strong president to lead the nation by himself? No.

It takes "We the people"
to make democracy succeed.

Thomas Jefferson said, "The will of the people is the only legitimate foundation of any government." The thought was echoed by John F. Kennedy: "There is no source of strength greater than the people of the United States: courageous, persevering, long-sighted."

We've already noted a paradox in American society. Our free, open, democratic system produces naturally creative people. But our authoritarian, domineering, competitive schools and workplaces reward people with logical and analytical skills.

As a nation, we face a great challenge. To compete with other societies, we need to make full use of the enormous store of creativity that exists within our population.

Since creative people function best
in open, democratic environments,
we need to develop a climate of
cooperation in education,
politics, and business.

You may say, "Charles, doesn't capitalism thrive best on competition? Doesn't it demand an authoritative chain of command? And how can you run a corporation if everybody acts like the boss?"

I learned part of the answer from Alan Ryan, professor of politics at Princeton University, who spoke to a class in business and government at Ohio State University's School of Public Policy and Management.

The theme of his presentation was that "participation is crucial to capitalism."

Ryan believes that if you run an enterprise simply as a system with profit being the only motive, you would end up with a population of unproductive opportunists, and "the whole system would go up with a loud bang." He said, "If you can't keep citizen self-control, you can't have capitalism either."

To make capitalism work, he contends, the citizen must be brought in as a participant. If the citizen is ignored and the "market" becomes the ultimate ruler, you end up with a harsh, authoritarian system.

Our national environment has bred a population of creative people ready to put their ideas and talents at the disposal of the economic system—if it's willing to use them.

Authoritarian governments do not have this rich resource. Their political and social environments breed "logical-thinking" populations, which are good at implementing ideas but less resourceful at generating them. If you have no ideas to implement, you have no progress.

A Conformist Culture

I have spent a significant amount of time working with Japanese companies and other Asian countries during a seven-year tenure as a specialist with the State of Ohio's Economic Development Department. My interaction with many company representatives and a lengthy visit to a steel company in Nagoya, Japan, helped me in understanding their culture.

My observations have led me to conclude that while the nation is a political democracy, its culture is rigidly authoritarian. In fact, if you take a close-up look Japan, you'll see a conformist society. The result is products and services of world-class quality and an individually personal interest to do their best. Their loyalty to their companies is remarkable. The autocratic culture works for them.

There is, however, a major difference worth noting. The Japanese develop companies for the good of their employees, whereas corporations in the United States are operated for the good of their stockholders.

The Japanese as well as many "Pacific Rim" Asian countries (including India, China, Indonesia, etc.) are logical thinking people and they are the toast of the economic world. They are leaders in automobile production, computers, electronics, and other manufacturing and service pursuits.

But as leading observers have pointed out, many Asian countries could not exist without America. They have achieved success by capitalizing on many creative ideas that may have been introduced elsewhere. The Asian industrial community has refined many of the ideas generated by Americans and Europeans and shipped them back to the innovators.

> *Problems are solved*
> *and ideas become reality*
> *when creative and logical people*
> *work together.*

The creative thinker comes up with a great idea, but before it's turned into reality, the innovator (creative thinker) puts it aside and moves on to another project. The logical thinker has few ideas, but follows through on most of them. People with such a thought process—the "Pacific Rim" Asian countries—profit by capitalizing on the creative thinkers "innovators" ideas.

The United States may have a potential advantage over the Pacific Rim countries because we are a nation filled with many dreamers. But when it comes to "doers" the Asian countries have Americans outnumbered by far.

As everyone knows, you create success by doing, not by dreaming. The Asian countries have discovered that, and are profiting by turning many American dreams into realities.

Elbow Room!

The Japanese have learned that conformity is the best way to get along on a crowded island. If you packed half the people in the United States into Montana, you'd have a population density comparable to Japan's, but Montana still has more usable land. When people live that close together they either develop rigid rules for behavior, and everyone must live up to them, or there is chaos. The United States, on the other hand, has a large population, but it still has huge areas of unused land.

A couple of centuries ago, when Daniel Boone looked out his cabin window and could see smoke from somebody else's chimney, he'd holler, "Elbow room!" and move on.

Old Daniel's neighbors never objected if he nailed coon-skins to the side of his cabin; they didn't live close enough to see them. They didn't care if he kept his hogs in a pen out back; they didn't live close enough to smell them. They didn't care if he put a lean-to on the back of his cabin so his mother-in-law could have her own separate quarters. That was Daniel's problem, not theirs.

The neighbors didn't even complain when he played his fiddle too loud. Fiddle music doesn't carry over a ridge and down a hollow.

Daniel knew, of course, that if his cabin caught fire, it

would be up to him and his family to put it out. If a band of Indians decided to steal his horse, it would be up to him to shoo them away. If he wanted a trail from his cabin to the nearest settlement, he would have to blaze it. If he fell over a cliff and broke a leg, he'd have to drag himself home and set it himself, with the help of his wife, Becky. If game got scarce, or he was unable to hunt, he'd have to live off wild greens, nuts, and berries—or go hungry. Such conditions breed independent, creative individuals.

What Are We Defending?

We have come a long way from the time of Daniel Boone. Now we have subdivisions, town houses, and apartment complexes. We also have zoning ordinances, building restrictions, building codes, noise abatement ordinances, and a variety of other regulations. There are fire regulations, police departments, emergency rescue squads, and highway administrations. We have workers compensation, unemployment benefits, Welfare, Social Security, Medicare and Medicaid—not to mention Blue Cross-Blue Shield.

We have developed cushions against catastrophe, and when we congregate in densely populated areas we have created orderly rules to keep us out of one another's hair. In one domain after another, we have traded independence for security. Order has been exchanged for spontaneity.

In our hearts and souls, however, we're still a nation of individuals. When you look at a crowd in Japan, you see Japanese. When you look at a crowd in the United States, you see Anglo-Saxons, African-Americans, Hispanics, Asians, Jews, Arabs, Italians, Slavs—a racial and ethnic mosaic.

We live under one federal Constitution, but we also have

fifty state constitutions, which grant varying degrees of autonomy to county and city governments. We adhere to hundreds of different religions. There are only two major political parties, but unlike their counterparts in European democracies, they don't demand rigid adherence to ideology. The Democratic party will embrace a conservative from Mississippi as well as a liberal from Massachusetts. The Republican Party will welcome a conservative from Arizona as well as a liberal from Connecticut.

> *The document that sets our national tone is not a restrictive code, but a liberating covenant.*

The Bill of Rights doesn't tell the individual what he *must* do; it tells the government what it *can't* do. We argue interminably over the things that lie between the lines of that document, but we'll take up arms to defend it in its totality. The Second Amendment gives us that right.

What are we defending? A nation whose greatest strength is people who work together.

In America, success is a two-letter word.

Say "*we*!"

8
Your New Environment

When I was an employee of Ohio State University and the State of Ohio, I was amazed at the rules and regulations. They had elevated the art of creating policy manuals to a new level.

One rule was taken especially seriously by those in charge: "No personal calls on state telephones." It was put into force because, in some cases, personal calls were abused.

Many members of the secretarial force were working mothers who dropped their children off at daycare centers on the way to the office. Because of the telephone rule, a mother who might have a reason to check on her child couldn't.

One secretary in particular had a daughter who was just getting over a virus. When I looked at her productivity, it was obvious that her mind was many miles away from her work.

"Barbara," I said, "Why don't you use my phone to see how she is doing?"

She dialed the number and said, "How's Melinda feeling?"

I could tell things were fine by the smile that broke like sunshine across her face.

For a thirty-second telephone call that didn't add a penny to the state budget, I had a rejuvenated, energetic secretary. To me, Barbara was not an employee, but a member of the team. Discretionary use of the phone was a morale builder.

The same principle that works in the office has applications to every area of life—in education, in politics, even in the life of a nation.

The "Five Guarantees"

In an authoritarian society, the subjected masses are molded by rules rather than by rewards. They know what is expected of them and fully understand the benefits of conformity and the penalties for nonconformity.

The Chinese Communist Party is a good example. It has been able to keep a billion people in subjection by providing the "five guarantees." In exchange for the obedience of the peasantry, it provides:

- Sufficient food
- Adequate clothing
- A basic shelter
- A secure retirement
- A decent burial

The people obey and the party provides.

What happened when the people rose in protest? They were terrified by tanks and bullied by bayonets. Such tactics don't produce a nation built on teamwork—but something just the opposite. The unity of the people lies just beneath the surface, waiting to explode.

The Communications Gap

The collapse of the Communist system can be laid at the feet of enforced orthodoxy.

When people's imaginations are stifled, and they are discouraged from free association with others who hold similar views, progress can't take place.

The Soviet school system taught its children the collective wisdom of Marx, Lenin, and Stalin. The teachings of those three were regarded as "holy writ" and the children could not venture beyond the boundaries. As it turned out, they might as well have been singing "Three Blind Mice."

A system so hostile to outside ideas discouraged communication. They seemed to ignore the fact that "communications technology" has been at the cutting edge of progress for the past generation. As a result of the system, Communist orthodoxy put the Soviets hopelessly behind in the computer revolution.

When we look at Japan, we see a different story. The Japanese might have been short on creative thinkers, but theirs was not an idea-proof society. They were smart enough to make use of creative ideas from outside.

It's not Japanese culture that has been exported, it is the technology. In Budapest, for example, the music piped into the department stores on a Sony system is more likely to be Johnny Cash than either Tchaikovsky or Liszt. Do you know any Japanese songs? The Hungarians don't know any either.

In today's world, trends start in the open societies of Europe and America where imaginative thinkers predominate. They catch on elsewhere, and the practical-minded analytical thinkers capitalize on them.

That's America—land of the free, home of the brave creative thinker who knows what can happen when people come together to brainstorm new ideas.

A Matter of Survival

Finally, America has realized that team processes with appropriate people involvement is the best option to accomplish continuous improvement and continued success. Over the years management and organizational strategies have come and gone, often called "fads." The one continuous survivor is process improvement through "teamwork and team processes."

Ziff-Davis's online *CIO Insight* magazine (CIOInsight. com) recently stated, "Radical re-engineering and other strategies may be as out of fashion as bell-bottoms and beehives, but business process improvement with appropriate teams to achieve improvement processes are still in vogue."

While some are straggling, most business leaders, educators and senior managers (public and private) continue to be on the bandwagon of team solutions to productivity and process improvement. Walls of division that existed for centuries are continuously being replaced by new environments with a spirit of cooperation and accomplishment.

> ### *Strategies for survival in the 21st century must include the joining of labor with management in the decision making process.*

The old-style "front office" authoritarian methods must be forever buried.

Some managers may find this new style threatening, but that should not be a surprise. People who are insecure feel intimidated when employees suddenly become "partners" of equal worth in the workplace. A manager who is afraid of what he or she does not understand may not grasp the true meaning of leadership. Instead of helping creative people use their natural talent, they clamp down on innovation. The result is an atmosphere of anxiety and pressure.

In the past, employees who constantly promoted extravagant ideas, tried different operating methods, or pursued independent hunches on company time were rarely tolerated. Today, managers usually complain that they are under pressure from top executives for short-term results and can't allow deviance from set goals or procedures. Yet when management is not supportive of its workers, productivity becomes sluggish.

Someone Who Cares

What is the answer? The key to a successful leadership system is an environment that encourages participation and a sense of belonging for all employees. Workers also need some sense of control over their tasks.

> *Teamwork requires a genuine*
> *caring for people and a willingness to*
> *not only give direction, but*
> *to listen to ideas.*

The leader should not be viewed as a "boss," but rather a facilitator of cooperation. As a worker at a textile mill in South Carolina put it, "I need to feel important and that my suggestions make a difference."

There is a hidden danger, however. A creative environment, established by good management practices, is very easy to destroy. If we do not constantly and carefully manage for imaginative input, or if individuals do not feel they are valued, an environment of negative tension and pressure is created.

Our response to what is happening in our three major environments—home, social, and work—affects everything we do. We can experience either affirmative or negative feelings in each of these areas. People who don't feel needed or important will ultimately show a steady decrease in productivity. But a "positive consistency" in these three environments will have a direct impact on improving both attitude and efficiency.

If employees are to work *with* management instead of *for* management, those in leadership need to be acutely aware of why employees act the way they do. A leader who is aware of the behavior patterns associated with stress, for example, can deal quite well with the people on his or her work team.

When an employee begins to exhibit aggressive behavior, how does management respond? In the traditional workplace, no one would take the time to determine whether the worker was under unusual pressure. They wouldn't seek to know the basic causes of the behavior. Instead, management would probably engage in some form of punishment to deal with the situation.

Uncaring discipline, more often than not, leads to grievances and antagonism. But the leader who shows a personal concern for the root causes of the actions of workers brings harmony to the workplace. Participative management leads to cooperation, creativity, and consensus.

It's Time to Begin

There are specific requirements for maintaining and enhancing a participative work environment:

- Leaders must be people-oriented.
- Management must encourage thoughts and ideas to be freely expressed for consideration.
- Emphasis must be placed on developing positive personal relationships.

- References to rank and status must be avoided.
- Common goals should be outlined, which can be attained through shared efforts.

While emerging management trends are somewhat easy to track, the greatest challenge is the need to train those who are charged with leadership responsibilities. An environment of cooperation can be realized if an intensive education plan is implemented to focus on team-building throughout the organization.

What about you?

Have you chosen teamwork to be your trademark? Is it your lifestyle? If not, it is time to put the skills we've been discussing into practice.

"Escaping the system" is not reserved for those under a totalitarian regime. You, too, may be bound by policies and procedures that stifle your progress—and the progress of those around you. Real change and transformation, however, is much closer than you realize.

When *you* decide to become a team player, it's surprising how quickly the world around you begins to change. You will soon realize that your new environment is much more than the work of one person.

Success is a team effort!

Bonus Chapter!

From bestselling *Creating A Culture of Success* by Charles B. Dygert, Ph.D. and Richard Jacobs, P.E.

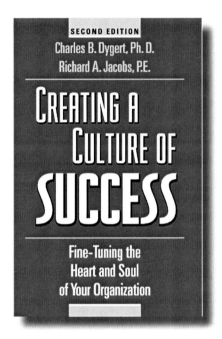

Creating A Culture of Success picks up where *Success Is A Team Effort* ends. Once you have your team dynamics in place, how far will you go without the proper environment in which to operate?

Here is a sample chapter from *Creating A Culture of Success*.

If you would like to purchase a copy, an order form is provided at the end of this book.

CULTURE DRIVES SUCCESS

Three forces drive performance and impact results: culture, leadership, and power. This book focuses on the first force: culture. Studied for centuries by anthropologists and archaeologists, culture involves rituals, symbols, and stories associated with a group of people. Culture offers a glimpse into people's beliefs and values—what's important to them and why. Beliefs and values are shaped by tradition, environment, and individual personalities. Culture, which drives behavior, amounts to the "clubhouse rules" or "the way we do things around here."

Typically, people who have been in an organization for a long time seek to preserve traditions while new employees seek to change the status quo. A culture of success endeavors to improve the old ways without losing the spirit of their traditions. How can a leader implement this healthy balance?

First, organizations must have a high level of *trust* among their members, and second, individuals within it need to have demonstrated personal *integrity*. Together, these form the foundation for a *shared fate*. Only when individuals in an organization embrace the principle of shared fate can they be on their way to a culture of success.

> **Shared Fate:**
> We win or lose,
> together.

Culture Shock

Unique societies exist inside every office building, manufacturing plant, and educational institution. For better or worse, each organization has its own working environment—complete with distinctive customs, rules, and regulations. Just as people often experience anxiety when moving to a new country, the same can be true when changing jobs. This anxiety is often due to what is called "culture shock." A recent client of ours experienced culture shock when he left Home Depot for a position at Microsoft. Although both are prominent Fortune 500 companies, their internal cultures are very different, and it took some time for him to learn and adjust to the new culture.

Unless you change jobs, you may be completely unaware of the impact culture has on your organization. Or, perhaps you are painfully aware of the negative effects of a culture in need of change. Regardless, one thing is certain. It will take time to learn and adjust to the culture. The sooner the organization begins that journey, the sooner you and the organization will find your road to success.

Another New Mandate?

Imagine transforming the heart and soul of your organization into one where quality is not simply a desired goal, but a lifestyle. The secret is getting employees involved. Studies as far back as 1992 have found that many improvement programs deliver shoddy results due to "marginal employee involvement levels." [1]

Despite the lip service that people are our best assets, companies continue to ignore their employees. Instead, they search for the silver bullet, the quick fix, or management tool-of-the-month. Why? Because mandating new policies is easier than taking time out to examine and improve the underlying culture.

Management often finds it easier to mandate new policies than take the time to examine and improve (or build an appropriate) the underlying culture.

If you want performance and results to flourish, if you want the competitive edge, it's time to explore your company's culture. Otherwise, quality and performance initiatives will merely irritate already beleaguered employees and become a bother to managers. Employees unable to internalize improvement processes being pushed on them, tend to perceive the orders for change as yet another scheme of assessment used to rank and rate everyone.

What's the Missing Link?

The missing link is having a clear understanding of the critical role that culture plays in the success of an organization. The culture of an organization is like the climate: it is present everywhere, yet mostly unnoticed until bad weather gets everyone's attention. The lack of a solid working culture inhibits real progress toward quality performance and results. If culture is not supporting the entire system, then an improvement program's technical and strategic segments are often rendered ineffective.

**Ingredients for a
Culture of Success:**
- ⬗ Trust each other
- ⬗ Have personal integrity
- ⬗ Agree on a shared fate

What fuels the culture of an organization? The management system (leadership). What influences the behaviors of those being led? The culture or organizational personality that management has activated, changed, altered, and challenged, based on its reactions to the existing cultural personality.

That brings us to a catch-22: If management exhibits no change in behavior or policies, the rank and file aren't going to initiate any change, either. Instead, management and nonmanagement will proceed to blame one another for any perceived problem.

If, however, both management and subordinates are involved in forming strategies on how to accomplish an improved culture (where trust and mutual interest thrive), the organization can begin to evolve in a positive way. *We* can solve problems together.

How Culture Impacts You

Sometimes, an illustration makes it easier to think about an old problem in a new way. In Figure 1.1 on page 18, Dr. Johnson Edosomwan illustrates the interplay between the management system and the employees' reactions.[2] In this diagram, generally known as the Edosomwan Model, four circles representing key systems in an organization (management, social, technical, and behavioral) revolve around a fifth circle of desired organizational changes.

Figure 1.1

Organizational and Process Transformation ("Edosomwan") Model

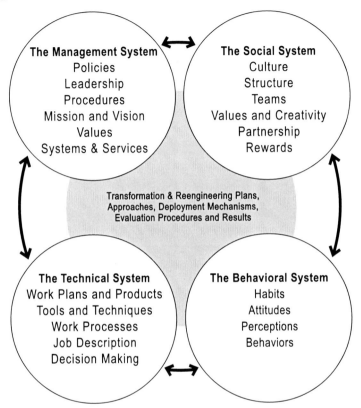

The lesson he drives home with this illustration is that all four systems—management, social, technical, and behavioral—are interlocked and mutually responsive to one another. Together, they hold the key to the evolution of the organization. Whatever transformation, right-sizing, process, or other improvements you wish to introduce in an organization, the success and effectiveness of that effort will be dependent on how the systems interact (the impact of the culture).

Of the four systems, note that the "management system" has the most power and impact on the other three systems. Culture and the change that management wants to effect are marked by a cause and effect relationship. Therefore, the vigilance of management in monitoring and interpreting the organization's behavioral trend, is essential in creating and maintaining a positive and productive organizational culture.

Just Another Scheme?

Demanding "higher standards" and "cooperation" to achieve quality products and services (or to increase productivity or profits) works temporarily if at all. A management demand spotlights a system characterized by the phrase, "Either I win or you lose!" This inspires workers to try to meet the expectations of an administrator or a supervisor – not to achieve excellent quality and productivity. Workers in such a system view themselves as doing the task for the boss, not the customer. Demands fuel internal competition which in turn spurs workers to do only enough to look better than the next person – in other words, just enough to get the supervisor off their backs.

Management *drives* culture.

Culture *drives* behavior.

Most of us would prefer a workforce that really cares about the success of the organization, and employees who take pride and ownership in the product or service they produce. When management attempts to introduce change, workers wonder, "Are they truly concerned about their workers, or is it merely a facade? Is a reward system in place to back up their promises? What is in it for me?"

A Way of Life

A culture of success is more than a technique for management to apply, more than a "program of the month" that employees can ignore and management can forget after a while. It's neither a simple tool nor a quick fix; it's a *way of life*. Employees in an internally competitive organization typically don't care whether their enterprise survives, and it shows. It's a sort of "get even" behavior that pits labor and management against one other.

The "we versus they" mentality fostered by traditional work environments needs to be turned inside out. The "we" should be your organization, and the "they" must become the competition. The good news is that it's easy to measure how much employees care. That's reflected by the amount of unprodded energy they put into their task.

It's Not New

More than two thousand years ago a Chinese warrior-philosopher by the name of Sun Tzu made essentially the same observation. In his classic book, *The Art of War,* Tzu stated:

> This is a matter of emptiness and fullness. When there are rifts between superiors and subordinates, when generals and officers are disaffected with each other and dissatisfaction has built up in the minds of the troops, this is called emptiness.
>
> When the civilian leadership is intelligent and the military leadership is good, when superiors and subordinates are of like mind, and will and energy operate together, this is called fullness.
>
> ...The skilled can fill their people with energy to confront the emptiness of others, while the incompetent drain their people of energy in face of the fullness of others.[3]

As leaders and workers in organizations, we must strive for "fullness." It is "like-mindedness" that produces certain victory. And, the sharing of a common goal—a shared fate—that builds a culture of success.

The Bag of Energy

Each morning we rise with a given quantity of strength and enthusiasm. Let's think of it as a bag of energy. As we prepare for the day's activities and travel to our workplace, we expend a certain amount of energy from our "bag." At our job, if we encounter anxiety or a negative attitude, that can drain so much energy that before mid-afternoon, we're empty and exhausted.

What, then, is left in our energy bag for our family and leisure activities? What happens to our quality of life? To gain maximum productivity in the workplace and beyond, we need leaders who ensure a positive environment. They help us conserve this energy. So once again, we reflect that the key to high output and positive employee morale rests with organizational culture and the management style.

Managers, fortunately, are waking up to the fact that workers are not robots in need of programming, but people with hearts, souls, and minds. Workers have feelings and emotions, and organizations that fail to acknowledge and address this are not treating employees as the full human beings they are. As authors Noel Tichy and Stratford Sherman note:

> Healthy people can't just drop their feelings off at home like a set of golf clubs. We are just beginning the search for ways to harness the vast power of workers' emotional energy.[4]

Beyond the Power Struggle

The value of working toward a system of total cooperation in the workplace has long been recognized, but only recently has it received the attention it deserves. What has prompted companies to sit up and take notice? Most organizations cite the increased global competition and recent economic challenges.

The biggest challenge in cooperative systems (introduced nearly seventy years ago by Christopher I. Barnard in *The Functions of the Executive*) is indoctrinating rank and file employees with a general sense of purpose, and granting them the ability to make major decisions.[5] Otherwise, how cohesive will the more detailed decisions be? Furthermore, if you allow executives to make decisions in isolation from workers, the organization runs the risk of losing touch with the essence of business, the customers and service or product produced. Misunderstandings and failure often result from not including front line employees in the decision process.

This challenge remains true today: If we don't work together, we're headed for failure. And to work together, we need to bring together four vital elements—often seen as opposing forces in an organization—into partnership. We call them the four "C's":

Change is one of those elements of life that you can always count on happening. In an organization, people struggle with change and each other because of change.

Competition, internal or external, impacts how people interact and how powerful (or not) those people are in a given situation.

Cooperation (often seen as the flip side of competition) can be an internal or external force that follows an individual's agenda or a team/company agenda. Cooperation can be a powerful force for good in an organization, as well as in the marketplace.

Control, and how control is granted, can be the power that makes or breaks an organization. Some situations call for more autocratic ("in charge") management methods and some require more democratic ("empowering") management methods. Autocratic leadership, where the person in authority tells everyone else what to do and how to do it, often results in people learning not to think for themselves and waiting until they are told what to do. This could lead to serious consequences for an organization as well as the individuals involved.

The traditional hierarchical management culture fuels the conflict among opposing forces:

Entity	Agenda	Opposing Forces
Organization	Survival	Market Competition
Owner	Wealth	Sharing with employees
Manager	Control	Empowering others

- The organization is trying to survive with strong competitors in the marketplace and trying to gain market share.

- The owner (stockholder) wants to keep as much wealth as possible from the company while the employees demand higher pay.

- And caught in the middle, we have managers trying to retain "control" while workers desire greater empowerment.

Recipe for Success

If this list reflects the realities of your organization, don't be discouraged. Being honest about where power resides is a first step toward forging a road map for new partnership. In traditional structures, authority emanates from a position, not a person. When power is misused in such a system, mistrust and fear arise. The fear is not just felt by employees; executives may experience fears of losing power, status, or compensation.

To move toward a new environment of achievement, both sides need to conclude that to get something, they have to give something. That "something" must be based on trust, personal integrity, and a shared fate. These are essential ingredients for creating a culture of success.

Who must take the first step? Leadership. Even with little assurance that employees will follow, leaders must persuade all sides to sit down together and "get used to each other." Leaders must lead the way if they are going to develop a culture of success.

Together they must:

- Become comfortable with new ideas
- Develop a strategy
- Cooperate on implementing a plan
- Test and evaluate results

That's the path that leads to a culture of success.

Key Concepts

1. Three forces drive performance and results: culture, leadership, and power.

2. Culture drives behavior, but it is management that must drive the culture.

3. Trust and integrity form the foundation of shared fate, which individuals must embrace to achieve a culture of success.

4. Employees are the missing link in most improvement programs.

5. Management often falls into a trap of mandating new policies and programs instead of taking the time to examine the underlying culture.

6. A win/lose culture (internally competitive workplace) motivates employees to do just enough to keep the supervisor off their backs.

7. Management, social, technical, and behavioral systems in an organization are interlocked and mutually responsive to each other. But, the management system has the most power over the other systems.

8. Having a common goal—a shared fate—unites people and helps you build a culture of success.

9. Management is responsible for creating and maintaining a positive work environment.

10. Organizations that fail to treat employees as human beings with hearts, souls, and minds will find performance and results deteriorate as the culture deteriorates.

Things To Do Now

1. Top level management must meet and make the commitment to examine the culture in their organization.

2. Next, all levels of management should gather together to discuss the concepts behind a culture of success and get feedback from lower and middle management on how best to involve the employees.

3. Open the channels of communication throughout the organization by having management and employees discuss the culture concepts.

4. A shared fate must be agreed upon. Begin the conversation to determine what that shared fate (common goal) will be.

5. If there's a "we versus they" internal competition mentality, convert it to "our company versus the market competition" approach (a shared vision).

6. Management should identify concrete ways to ensure a positive work environment. How can policies and procedures be changed to treat employees more as human beings and less like machines?

7. Ensure that workers make some major decisions and have a clear sense of purpose.

8. Ask employees for ideas on how to improve the culture and quality of products/services.

About the Author

Charles B. Dygert, Ph.D., C.P.A.E., C.P.S., began his career as a tool & die maker for General Motors. He earned his bachelor, masters, and doctorate from The Ohio State University and served on its faculty for nineteen years.

For seven years of his university career, Dr. Dygert served as a management specialist with the Ohio Department of Development's Economic Development Team, the same group that brought Honda of America to Ohio.

A past president of the Ohio Speakers Forum, Dr. Dygert is a Certified Speaking Professional (CPS) and is one of 195 professionals world-wide that has been awarded the Council of Peers Award for Excellence (CPAE) by the National Speakers Association. As a consultant and speaker, he has made presentations to over 2,500 businesses and organizations in all fifty states and several foreign countries.

Dr. Dygert authored this bestselling book, *Success Is A Team Effort*, and partnered with Richard Jacobs in authoring the acclaimed book *Creating a Culture of Success*. President and founder of MEI, International, Dr. Dygert is currently serving as an Adjunct Faculty member for Franklin University's School of Business M.B.A. program.

He and his wife, Donna, live in Columbus, Ohio. When not teaching, mentoring, or advising, Charles can be found piloting an aircraft—his other passion in life.

Quick Order Form

📠 Fax this form to: 845-987-7845

☎ Telephone: 845-987-7750
 (have your credit card ready)

💻 Email orders: orders@KeeneBooks.com
 (or order online at www.KeeneBooks.com)

✉ Postal Orders: Keene Books PO Box 54 Warwick, NY 10990

☐ **YES**, please send me the following:

	QTY	PRICE	TOTAL
Culture of Success	_____	X $19.95 =	_____
Success Is A Team Eff.	_____	X $10.00 =	_____
Shipping & Handling			__FREE__
Sales Tax (NY and PA only)			_____

Total Amount Due = _____

Payment Method

☐ Check ☐ Visa ☐ MasterCard ☐ Amex ☐ Discover
Please make checks payable to **Keene Publishing**

Card Number: _____ Exp. Date: ___/___

Security Code: _____ (usually on back of card)

Name (print): _____ Signature: _____

Organization: _____

Billing Address: _____

City: _____ State: _____ Zip: _____

Note: If you would like to have books shipped to a different address than your billing address, please provide that address on the back of this form or on a separate page.

Thank you for your order!

Share The Journey

Tell Us Your Story

We hope that this book has inspired you and your organization to replace internal competition with teamwork and cooperation. We invite you to share your story with us as you embark on this journey to success. Tell us what obstacles you faced, what methods worked and which concepts did not hold true for you. We will gather this information and incorporate it into the next edition. Help us "raise the bar" for future readers.

Send your culture of success story, feedback, comments, and suggestions to:

Success Is A Team Effort

Keene Publishing

PO Box 54

Warwick, NY 10990

Or, write comments below and fax to 845-987-7845:

_____

_____

_____

_____

_____

Thank you

Want to share *Success Is A Team Effort* with someone or get your own copy of *Creating A Culture of Success*?
Use the **Quick Order Form** on the back of this page!
Free Shipping! Bulk order discounts available.